Sip, Pick, and Pack...

Put the buzzback
in gardening !

Sip, Pick, AND Pack...

How Pollinators Help Plants Make Seeds

Polly W. Cheney

Written by **Polly W. Cheney**

Illustrated by **Kim Overton**

ORANGE *frazer* PRESS

Wilmington, Ohio

ISBN 978-1939710-550
Copyright©2017 Polly Winterbottom Cheney
All Rights Reserved

Published for the author by:
Orange Frazer Press
P.O. Box 214
Wilmington, OH 45177

Telephone: 937.382.3196 for price and shipping information.
Website: www.orangefrazer.com

Book and cover design: Alyson Rua and Orange Frazer Press

Library of Congress Control Number: 2016952458

Printed in China
67271-0

First Printing

Thank you to Master Gardener educators, volunteers, and Garden Club members everywhere who strive to improve horticultural practices in their communities. Special thanks to John and Ben Cheney and also to educators Kim Overton, Susan Theiss, Phoebe Crandall, Beth Mosshart, Suzi Winterbottom, Stephen Wallace, and Debbie Dolan.

Seed-making powers!

1

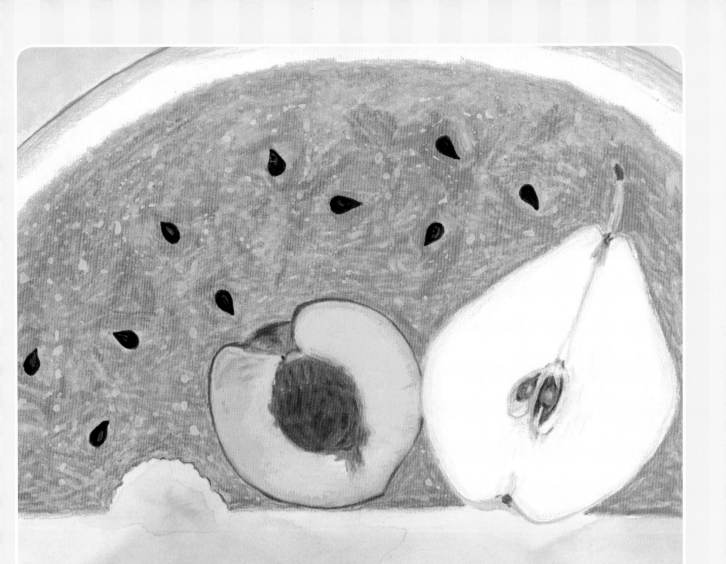

When it's time to grow plants for the food that we need,
Most plants that we grow will be started from seed.

Where does a seed come from? How does a seed start?
In a seed's early life, who plays a big part?

To answer these questions we'll visit some flowers
And take a quick look at their seed-making powers!

A seed's like a suitcase that's all packed to go.
It carries what's needed for new plants to grow.

It carries taste and texture, as well as root and stem.
They are all packed inside. We just cannot see them.

Some seeds are huge, others tiny as dust,
But before seeds get *packed*, plants get ready. They must!

poppy   popcorn   pumpkin   lima bean   avocado

We know plants are ready when their flowers unfold,
And that is the start, as our story is told.

With flowers in bloom, some plants have all they need
To finish the job of *packing* their seeds.

But for many more plants some supplies may be lacking.
These plants will need help with their *moving* and *packing*.

4

Blueberry Bee

Gulf Fritillary

Bumble Bee

Florida Carpenter Ant

If what they need
Is within, or next door,
The plants that need help
Attract pollinators!

Who are these helpers
Who pollinate plants?
Some you may know,
Like bees, butterflies, ants...

Honey Bee

Black and White Ruffed Lemur

Lesser Long-nosed Bat

Gecko

Green Beetle

Hummingbird

Birds, bats, and moths
Are some others with wings.
Even lemurs and beetles
Help plants *pack* their things!

But, why do they help?
Are they just in the mood?
No! The reason they help is...
They're looking for food.

And flowers have food—world class and first rate!
Pollen is protein! Nectar? Carbohydrate!

And flowers' bright colors and shapes look like signs
That advertise: "Pollinators! Please come here to dine!"

They come to find food, but they do something greater,
Which is how they have come to be called pollinators.

Ruby-throated Hummingbird

Acmon Blue Butterfly

Bumble Bee

Polly's Produce
Farm Fresh Market
JUST AHEAD

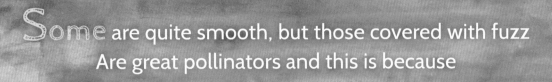

Some are quite smooth, but those covered with fuzz
Are great pollinators and this is because

The hairs on their bodies help pollen to stick,
So carrying pollen is not a hard trick.

The powder-like pollen at first can be found
On the anthers, 'til pollinators move it around.

Western Honey Bee

Covered with fuzz!

8

helping plants

Western Honey Bee

Some bees will pick pollen to make a *bee bread*.
Other pollinators will sip the plant nectar instead.

But both pickers and sippers help plant pollen scatter,
So flowers get pollen *packed* right where it matters.

For when pollen is placed, on just the right spot,
(On the stigma in the pistil) it **helps** plants a lot.

When pollen's on the stigma, we call that *pollination*,
It may tunnel through the style, like a train into a station,

It goes into the ovary, just what the ovule needs.
That's "fertilization!" The ovule becomes a seed!

Once seeds are packed, they grow 'til they're ripe.
Until they can move to grow plants of their type.

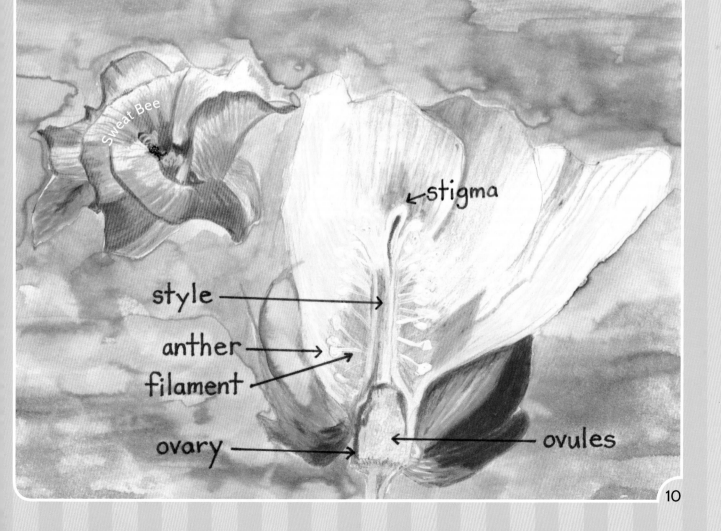

Sweat Bee

stigma

style

anther

filament

ovary

ovules

New plants grow more seeds,
Yes, and vegetables! Fruits!
Some seeds we eat!
We eat tops! We eat roots!

But our food grown from plants
Doesn't come to us free.
It costs money and time,
And hard work is the key.

Growers and farmers plant, water, and weed,
To help grow the plants for the food that we need.

All kinds of farmers would share a sad fate,
If pollinators weren't able to help pollinate.

There's one pollinator here in the U.S.—
A species whose habits are some of the best.

And though in The States they're not native at all,
When big crops need help, honey bees get a call.

Beekeepers bring them from miles away
To pollinate crops—the right week, the right day.

BEES 4HIRE

When trees are in bloom, the bees *work* the flowers.
They feed and move pollen, for hours and hours.

Those farmers whose trees fill with almonds or fruit,
Don't think of these bees as just fuzzy and cute.

The work these bees do helps the farmers make money,
While bees fill their hives with more bees and more honey.

It is also amazing, as researchers state,
That the number of native bee species is great.

Most states have hundreds of species of bees—
Hard working, mild mannered, pollinating with ease.

Most *natives* do not nest in hives, but are found
In tunnels in trees. Some nest underground.

Some nest underground!

Digger Bee tunnels

Leaf Cutter Bee

Miner Bee

The work that they do is more than just *buzz*.
If we can help them, we should! That is because

Without their good help we would be without crops,
And some crops we have that are good, would be flops!

Sunflower Bee

Tri-colored Bumble Bee

Green Sweat Bee

Squash Bees

Mason Bee

One way we can help is to keep some ground clear,
And not mulch every inch of our gardens each year.

We can also protect them from chemical harm,
To keep the food coming to tables from farms.

If we spray to kill pests at the right time of day,
Pollinators may safely be out of harm's way.

We can protect them!

And if we kill weeds, in addition to pests,
Pollinators' favorites might be killed with the rest.

So, protecting our pollinators includes, of course,
Letting them find their favorite food source!

By protecting them and their food, as we should,
We'll help them continue their work and that's good!

So let's raise a cheer for the work that they do!
To grow lots of food, we need more than a few!

May millions and millions find good *food and drink*!
They make a big difference! Much more than you'd think!

Raise a cheer!

Monarch Butterflies

19

Shoulder-to-shoulder and wing-to-wing,
We can help one another grow many great things!

Glossary

Carbohydrate: Carbohydrates are groups of hydrogen and carbon atoms in our foods which give us energy.

Crop: Crops are plants that we grow and harvest for food.

Fruit: Fruit is the part of a plant that surrounds its seeds. Fruit develops from a plant's flower. Tomatoes, cucumbers, pumpkins, and squash are fruits.

Native: A native plant or a native insect is one that is naturally found in an area.

Pest: A pest is an insect or other animal that attacks crops, food, or farm animals.

Pistil: The pistil is the part of a flower that the pollen gets moved to in order to form a mature seed. It contains the stigma, style, the ovary and ovules.

Pollen: A fine powdery substance produced by plants as part of the seed-making process.

Protein: Proteins are groups of carbon, hydrogen, oxygen, and nitrogen atoms found in some foods which we need for our bodies to grow.

Species: A species is a specific group of plants or animals that has many shared physical characteristics and qualities.

Stamen: The stamen is the part of a flower that supports the pollen. It contains the filament and the anther.

Vegetable: A vegetable is the edible part of a plant that does not contain seeds. Celery (a stem), carrot and beet (root), and broccoli (stem and bud) are vegetables.

Weed: A weed is a wild plant that grows where it is not wanted. In the right places, wild plants are valued for their flowers, fruits, the shade they provide, and for other benefits.

Fun Facts

Importance of pollinators—About ⅓ of all crops depend on pollinators. The National Pollinator Garden Network says we should, "thank pollinators for 1 out of every 3 bites of food we eat."

Some crops that need pollinators—Alfalfa, almond, apple, apricot, blackberry, blueberry, cherry, clover, cranberry, cucumber, cantaloupe, nectarine, peach, pear, plum, pumpkin, raspberry, squash, sunflower, and watermelon.

Some crops that benefit from pollinators—Eggplant, grape, lima bean, okra, pepper, soybean, and strawberry.

Some crops that do not need or benefit from pollinators—Sweet corn, wheat, rice, oats, rye, walnut, pecan, cabbage, broccoli, and spinach.

Night time pollinators—Most bats, lemurs, and moths pollinate at night. Bats pollinate over 300 species of fruit.

Day time pollinators—Birds, butterflies, and bees pollinate primarily during the day.

What are some native bees?—Bumble bees, carpenter bees, digger bees, leaf cutter bees, miner bees, mason bees, and sweat bees are common in most of the United States. The Western honey bee naturally occurs in Europe, Africa, and the Middle East. It came to the U.S. with early settlers in about 1622. There are about 20,000 species of bees worldwide.

What is a bee keeper?—Bee keepers are people who provide houses, called hives, for groups of bees, called colonies. Bees will pollinate crops within a few miles of their hives.

Do bees like to sting?—Some bees sting to protect their hives or nests. Most bees do not sting. If you stay calm when you see a bee and do not move quickly around them, most bees will stay focused on their work.

Test what you've learned with a fun crossword puzzle at:
www.crosswordhobbyist.com/151533
password: sipandpick

The Pollen's Path

If
you want
to know the way
the *pollen* went, it started
on the *anther* on the *filament*. These
parts of the *stamen* start the *pollen* on its way,
although it starts here we hope it doesn't stay. It needs
to reach the *pistil: stigma, style* and the O's (the *ovary* and *ovules*)
so this is how it goes—Perhaps a bee should brush some *pollen* while
he feeds, if it falls onto the *pistil*, it can help to pack the *seed*. With
pollen on the *stigma* (we call that step *pollination*) it can tunnel through
the *style* and like a train into a station it arrives inside the *ovary*, that's
what the *ovule* needs (that's *fertilization*). The *ovule* becomes a *seed*.
The *seed* will grow there until it is *ripe*, until it can move to grow *plants*
of its type. Some *seeds* will be moved by the wind or the rain, or
by man or by beast, they don't travel in vain. When a *seed* finds
a spot where conditions are right the *seed* will unpack
and o'er days and o'er nights a *root*
will dig down to keep it secure.
A *stem* will unfold for
growth to be
sure.

Bibliography

Baldock, Katherine, et.al. "Where is the UK's Pollinator Biodiversity? The Importance of urban areas for flower-visiting insects." *Proceedings of the Royal Society of London B*, February 11, 2015. http://www.academia.edu/10749395/Where_is_the_UKs_pollinator_biodiversity_The_importance_of_urban_areas_for_flower-visiting_insects.

Skinner, John, Ph.D. "If Flowers are Restaurants to Bees, What are Bees to Flowers?" *All Bugs Good and Bad Webinar Series*. Alabama Cooperative Extension System. February 7, 2014. http://articles.extension.org/pages/70120/all-bugs-good-and-bad-2014-webinar-series.

Isaacs, Rufus. "Smart Gardening for Bees and Other Pollinators." Webinar, Michigan State University Extension Smart Gardening Program. October 4, 2013. http://msue.anr.msu.edu/resources/smart_gardening_for_pollinators_webinar.

About the Author & Illustrator

Polly Winterbottom Cheney was the third of five children born to parents who loved reading to their children and who appreciated and loved the out-of-doors. Her interest in gardening was nurtured by her husband, John Cheney, whose passion for gardening came from his mother and grandmother. After countless landscaping projects together, and even after studying pollinators in Master Gardening courses, while Polly appreciated and celebrated their role in seed production, she had never really met a pollinator she liked. That changed with her introduction to native pollinators. Realizing that native plants have ongoing relationships with specific (local) pollinators increased her appreciation for the garden as a community—full of magnificent, edible art and local pollinator patrons. She looks forward to learning more about these patrons as she works alongside John and their son, Ben, in Horton Bay, Michigan.

Kim Overton's art career began in 7th grade, when someone purchased her purple papier-mâché hippopotamus which was wearing white lace-up sneakers. In the intervening years, she opened a bookstore, coached gymnastics, raised five children, co-founded an arts-integrated K–12 school, taught math and art, served as the elementary principal for the International School of Ouagadougou in West Africa, and taught homeschool families. Kim lives near the shores of Lake Michigan with a big dog named Milo, who traveled back from Africa with her. She has seen that the earth is full of glorious, astounding, breathtaking, curious works of art, and her goal with her artwork is to celebrate the magnificence of nature.